THE LIFE OF LITTLE NICK

Copyright © 2022 Nicholas De Graaf

All rights reserved.

No part of this publication may be reproduced, distributed or transmitted in any form, or by any means, including photocopying, recording or other electronic or mechanical methods, without the prior written permission of the publisher, except in the case of brief quotations embodied in reviews and certain other noncommercial uses permitted by copyright law.

The moral right of the author and illustrator has been asserted.

Story by: Nicholas De Graaf
Illustrations by: Miguel Smith G
Edited by: Chris Stead
Published by: MAWS
Design: Chris Stead, Old Mate Media | www.oldmatemedia.com

For orders and more info, please visit: www.mawsgroup.com.au

Paperback ISBN-13: 978-0-6454734-0-7
Hardcover ISBN-13: 978-0-6454734-1-4
Digital ISBN-13: 978-0-6454734-2-1

What is MAWS?

The titular Little Nick is now an adult and the founder of MAWS Group. Its focus is on combining mental awareness with sports. MAWS teaches kids and adults how to surf, skate and bodyboard whilst raising awareness for mental health. Follow MAWS on Instagram or Facebook or head over to the website.

www.mawsgroup.com.au

Clarkson Skatepark

There once was a boy
named Nicholas.
He was born with
so much energy.
It seemed endless.

Nick had to do something with
all this energy.
Which is why he loved to skate.
His friends tried to keep up,
but they always needed a break.

He found it very hard
to concentrate at school.
Sitting still in one spot,
not able to do a lot.

So after school,
it was time to skate.
Hours and hours of practise.
Until it was very, very late.

Leederville Skatepark

Once he burned all his energy,
it was time to rest.
It was skating that always helped him,
sleep the best.

Even on those days
when he awoke feeling sad.
He found energy from his skating,
and the best times he ever had.

Because skateboarding
made Nick smile.
So the sad feeling only lasted
a little while.

Plus his classmates at school,
all thought he was cool.
So he made new mates,
who also loved to skate.

Carine Skatepark

Practising new tricks,

Nick would fall a bit.

And eventually sprained his ankle pretty bad,

which wasn't rad.

Nick wasn't going to

skate for a while.

So his sad days,

began to build into a terrible pile.

Nick wondered... if he couldn't skate again
How would he be able to fix
his upset brain.

brain

The doctor told him
To take up swimming
But that didn't give
the same great feeling.

What if Nick could
skate on water.
The falls won't be as bad!
And maybe it would help Nick,
not feel so sad.

So, Nick picked up a surfboard
and journeyed
to the ocean.
Learning to surf wasn't so hard.
All he had to do was feel the motion.

He eventually got to his feet
and rode his first wave.
Paddling in to the big blue sea,
he had to be brave.

He practised in many conditions,
seeking the perfect board to ride.
He wanted to be inside the wave,
with a barrel
around him on every side.

One weekend morning,
that day came.
And with it, happiness,
to his upset brain.

He rode down the wave's face,
stalling so he could go slower.
As the blue curled over,
and became his water enclosure.

Nick was inside the barrel,
as time stood still.
He knew he was hooked!
It was the ultimate thrill.

He had found another sport,
that made him smile.
Now all those sad days,
couldn't build into a pile.

He had found the ultimate feeling.

It was inside the barrel
of a wave.

But getting barrelled on a surfboard
was tough.

The waves weren't always big enough.

He saw that his friends would lay down

on a bodyboard,

And pull straight into a barrel.

Nick wanted to try this,

as he was obsessed with barrel bliss.

Bodyboarding meant every wave
could give Nick a barrel.
And each barrel made him smile.

So, now he had two more options
to treat the sad days,
and knock down that pile.

Nick was born with a mental illness
and a life too filled with
highs and lows.

His lows would cause an upset brain

But now he knew how to get back his smile again

He would just choose his desired board and train.

The Life of Big Nick

Top: Getting barrelled on a bodyboard in Bali.

Middle: Frontside alleyoop at Clarkson Skatepark.

Bottom: Surfing inside a Scarborough barrel.

As an adult, Nick focusses on his happiness by spending time with his family, surfing, skating, bodyboarding and building.

He found over the years that having a certain amount of happiness in his life, reduces his stress levels and maintains his mental health with a combination of appropriate medication.

Pictured in this photo is just some of the kids that Nick has taught through MAWS group.

www.ingramcontent.com/pod-product-compliance
Lightning Source LLC
Chambersburg PA
CBHW061135010526
44107CB00068B/2954